MY
FAILURES
MOTIVATED
MY
SUCCESS

MY
FAILURES
MOTIVATED
MY
SUCCESS

JOSEPH CARNEY

PTP

Pure Thoughts Publishing, LLC

Table of Contents

Dedication

This book is dedicated to Jamellah (Fiancé), Chematal (Mom), Joseph (Dad), Shamyriah (Sister), Jasmine (Sister), and Sammie (Great-Grandfather) For always supporting me through my faults and failures. For helping me grow into the man I have become today. For loving me unconditionally even when I wasn't sure how to love myself. For teaching me how to be a man. For being my shelter and pushing me to achieve the greatness you engraved in me. I love you!

Preface

Everyone in life goes through trials. It is important to understand you can overcome any adversity you go through. Fear consumes us to a point that we cannot recognize ourselves. The one thing in life you know you're good at and have given your full commitment to is hard to let go for any period of time. Once that is gone, your life seems like it's a waste. What is the breaking point for you to find your happiness again? How can you overcome the barriers and obstacles you will face? When everything around you seems dark, what will guide you to the light again?

My trials and obstacles were my fault. I didn't understand how to deal with certain situations and the darkness consumed me. My story is a reality of what happens when life has no guidance. When you lose a portion of your life that made you happy, how can you move forward? I want my failures to be lessons for students and athletes around the world. It is important to help others in any way you can. Although I failed, it was only temporary. I never once believed any of my circumstances were permanent, but I made all the wrong decisions while I was in those situations. This book is for any athlete, student, young adult, or anyone who is facing situations that seem too big for them to handle. My reality now is different from my reality then and overcoming the adversity I faced can hopefully help others achieve their dreams as well. Whatever you're suppressing or struggling to handle, jump out on faith, and reclaim your passion. Nothing lasts forever, enjoy it while you can.

Introduction

Going to college was not a big tradition in my family. There was always a choice of getting a job or going to college. However, making good grades and being great at whatever you do has always been a priority. It was always known, nothing was more important than education, especially not sports. We weren't a big religious family, but God has always been the head of our house and our lives. Sometimes that was forgotten when you put so much on yourself and nothing seems to go your way. In the blink of an eye, your whole life can change, but what will be your breaking point?

I worked hard to become a model student and football player. I always kept God first and pushed myself to be great. God blessed me in many ways throughout my high school career, academically, and athletically. I received many accolades and achieved things I never dreamed about. All of my efforts were to prepare myself to play college football. Just as every young athlete dreamed of doing, I wanted to play professionally. I knew those chances were slim, but I worked daily to get better. When I started getting accepted into colleges, I was overly excited, but I still wanted an offer to play football. I didn't care where, but I wanted to play. I was able to get this chance and I was eager to take that step.

Getting a chance to play college football was a dream come true. I loved the campus and the facilities we used. The players were great and some of them have become brothers to me. I wanted to be known as a role model for the generation after me in my hometown. Just as I did in high school, I worked tediously to become a better player and keep my grades up in college. However, as time passed, I began to realize the dream I had of college football was not the reality of college football. The love for the game began to slip away from me slowly. I never imagined not wanting to play the game I grew up loving more than anything. Somehow, it came to a point where I didn't want to fully commit myself to the game anymore. Football has always been paired with my success academically. I knew I needed to keep my grades in good standing if I wanted to play football. If football was not going to be a part of my life anymore, what would happen to me academically?

I was in a new space in my life because the one thing everyone could identify me by was gone. I had to make a new name for myself. The entire time I was going through this dilemma, it seemed as though I threw God away. I transferred schools to start a new journey, but I never thought I would be in a place where I didn't recognize myself anymore. Without football, my life took a turn for the worse and I was fighting to get back on track. Failure after failure, and tragedy after tragedy consumed my life. I wasn't able to focus or be my best self. My reality was converted to laziness, unhappiness, withdrawals from society, and lies. I didn't know who I was, and I couldn't stand the path I was going down.

My breaking point came when I realized I couldn't depend on my own strength and knowledge to solve my problems. I knew I needed to give my life to God again and allow him to guide me. Greatness was always instilled in me as a child, but I had to realize it was always in me to get out of my head. Even through failures and loss, I was able to focus and get back to the Joseph I knew myself to be.

CHAPTER 1

Kickoff

My last year of high school is finally here. I have been working hard for this year to go out with a bang, athletically and academically. I did not like school until I got to high school and it was almost over. My joy all through high school was playing football, lifting weights with my friends, and being with my girlfriend. She was very supportive of me and always motivated me to be great at whatever I did. School always came easy to me and in my earlier years I did not push myself as I should have, but I always stayed on the honor roll. I knew my grades had to stay good in order for me to continue playing football in high school and hopefully college. My mom and dad definitely did not play any games when it came to school work. They pushed me to be committed, have perseverance, be respectful, and always give

100% no matter what. I took this mentality in every aspect of my life. Once my senior year got here, I was prepared to unleash these morals and values tenfold on academics and football.

Football has always been my passion since I was eight and I was determined to be the best version of myself to go on and play college football. Every day on the field I worked my butt off. Everyone who supported me always pushed me to make sure I did not settle or become complacent. I wanted to be great and they expected greatness from me. I always prayed before every game and thanked God before and after practices. There was never a time, I did not give my entire body and soul to the game of football. God gave me courage and bravery every day to do what I love and give my all in those areas. I stayed on top of my grades and performed well during the season. I won player of the week twice during the regular season and even made an appearance on television as player of the week. I pushed myself to the limit time and time again to achieve the results I wanted. I knew without the help of God, none of this would be possible.

Once the regular season was over, my teammates and I worked tediously to go to a state championship. We played extremely well, but we lost in the third round of the state playoffs. I never cried as much as I did during that last game of my high school career. My mother and my little sister Jasmine sat on the field with me while my eyes bled with pain and disappointment. I felt like all my hard work had been in vain. Little did I know, God had other plans for me once the season was over. A few days passed, and the pain finally began to subside. My head coach called me into his office the next week to talk with me. He told me I had been nominated for player of the year from two different hosts, I was named scholar-athlete of the year in the entire area, I was also voted one of the best linemen in our conference. I came in second for the player of the year in our area, but I won WLTX player of the year against a lot of good competition. Although I had not won a state championship with my friends, I had achieved awards for all the hard work I put in on and off the field. In all of my speeches, I thanked God first and foremost and I thanked my teammates. Without having a support system that held me accountable at all times and keeping God first in everything I did, I would not have achieved the accomplishments I did that year.

Now that football was over, I was just a normal student for the first time since I was seven and it was time to work towards finishing strong for graduation. My senior year was definitely my easiest academic year of high school. My workload was small, and I was able to gain some experience in my career field. My goal was to become an interior designer. My business applications teacher convinced me I should go into education because I was a good leader and she noticed people loved to be around me. I never once considered being a teacher until she came to me about it. I went on through the semester taking the classes I needed and finished on the honor roll for the first semester. Once the second semester came, I did not need a lot of classes. Mrs. June was our guidance counselor and she put me in a few classes to pass time being that I had all my credits for graduation. No, we did not have early dismissal during these years. As the old saying goes, God works in mysterious ways. My first block class, which was English five, got terminated. I went into Mrs. June's office to find a new class I could take. She recommended enrolling in teacher cadet. I never considered this would be a possibility for me. She convinced me to take teacher cadet and I agreed.

Being in this program was definitely the start of a new beginning for me. I was the only male in the class, and I was able to learn a lot from my female peers about education. In order to pass this class, we had to complete an internship. I wanted to work at the middle school because I was not too thrilled to teach young students. However, I ended up doing my hours in a 4k setting. This experience was definitely interesting. I was not prepared to be in a classroom with a group of young students at all. My football mentality did not allow me to be loving and caring as I should have been with those students. My teacher had a one on one conversation with me about my approach in the classroom and how I could improve. She wanted me to be more subtle and interactive with the students. In the coming days, I had to teach a lesson to the students, so the talk was just in time. Over the duration of the internship, I began to interact with the students more and help in the classroom as much as I could. Besides football, this was by far the best experience I had in high school. It was my first time being outside my comfort zone and the beginning of me becoming a new person.

Along with staying on top of my grades and gaining the new experiences teacher cadet brought, I also was able to talk with about four or five colleges. I really wanted to attend North Carolina A&T University. I went on a visit with some players the previous year and I fell in love with the school. The campus was beautiful, exciting, and the culture was just like my high school. The head coach came to Lee Central and talked with me and one of our tailbacks. I did not receive any offers from any school, but I knew I really wanted to play football on the next level. I prayed every day and continued to work hard to stay in shape for the upcoming season. About a month after I met with the coach from North Carolina A&T, I still had not received any offers. My head coach started calling different schools for me and he found a school that was just starting a football program for the upcoming season. He told the coach about me and I was able to go to this school along with the running back who was with me when I was talking to the North Carolina A&T coach. This was a dream come true, I dreamt of this opportunity all my life and the chance finally came. All my hard work paid off and I was on my way to becoming a college football player.

The school year was over, and it was time for graduation. I finished number fourteen in my class, a 3.8 GPA, and received many scholarships to attend the college or university of my choice. None of this would have been possible without keeping God first and working hard to achieve my dream. I was able to complete the financial aid process and get ready for enrollment into my new home for the next four years. At least that's what I thought.

CHAPTER 2

First and Ten

Limestone was definitely not my first, second, or third choice. In fact, I asked myself, what the hell is a Limestone anyway? I never heard of this school before, but they were willing to give me an opportunity and I was grateful for that. I knew I wanted to play football and I did not care where. Limestone was just starting a football program and I felt this was a perfect opportunity to play early and get a good education. Once my head coach got off the phone with the assistant head coach from Limestone, I needed to apply to the school and get accepted. My grades and test scores were pretty good, therefore, I was not worried about being accepted. I waited with anticipation to receive a letter from the school. I received my acceptance letter about a week after I applied, and I was beyond excited. My dream was slowly becoming a reality. I was awarded scholarships from the school and I had scholarships I could use from the state due to my GPA and test scores. Once I knew I was accepted, I contacted the football coach to let him know. He gave me specific instructions on what I needed to do next. I had to go to the school on a Saturday with my parents to meet all the coaches, take my placement tests, and get a tour of the campus. This visit was an eye-opening experience for me. This was the first time in my life I was ever stereotyped.

When I stepped on Limestone's campus I was filled with joy and eagerness. The campus was small, but I could feel the positive energy from the campus. When we parked our car and began to walk around, there were people directing us to the cafeteria for the beginning of the visitation process. Once we entered the cafeteria, there were professors, faculty workers, and students who talked with us about the school, their experiences, and the great amenities the school and community had to offer. Once they finished giving their brief introductions, we were split into groups to finish the tour. My first stop on the tour was to take my placement tests. These placement tests were used to determine what classes I would take once I began in the fall semester. I walked in the computer lab filled with confidence. I have always been a good test taker and I never worry about the results because there is always a way to overcome obstacles. There were three tests I had to take, math, reading, and writing. The questions were easier than I thought they would be. I was maybe the second one to finish all three tests and submit my scores to the instructor. I did not score as well as I should have on the math portion, but I breezed through the reading and writing tests. When I walked over to the instructor to give him the paper with my grades, he looked at me with a puzzled face. I stood there waiting for him to tell me what I needed to do next, but I did not expect what happened next. He held his hand out still looking puzzled and said to me, "Son I must apologize to you. When you walked in, I immediately said to myself, oh he is here for football and he won't do very well on these tests and will be in remedial classes. These are some of the best grades I have seen all weekend by far. You should go and talk with the director of the math department and ask to retake the math portion because with these grades I know you will ace it if you had another opportunity." I can honestly say for the first time in my life I was baffled. Here I was an eighteen-year-old kid who has done his very best in school all of his life being stereotyped because I was big, black, and assumed to be at a college campus because of my football talents. I knew about stereotypes as well as racism, but I did not expect it to happen during this experience. When he said those words to me, I looked him in his eyes and said, "Well sir I don't know where you come from, but where I come from we take pride in our education and my parents have pushed me to be the best version of myself in all aspects of life. You have a great day." Once I finished my statement, I walked out of the computer lab in disbelief and awe. I am optimistic in all situations and that situation did not change my optimism. I am confident in myself and who I am, and this situation just gave me extra fuel to be great.

Once I left the computer lab and was back with my parents, I told them what transpired. They were in complete shock and could not believe it. They thought I was joking, but they knew who they raised, and they were proud of how I handled the situation. Yes, they wanted to confront the professor. However, I thought it would be more important to simply be great when I got on campus in the fall. The next part of the visit was a tour of Gaffney. This was the community Limestone was located in. Gaffney was known for its high school being great at football. They produced a few NFL players and won a lot of high school state championships. A lot of their players were pretty good, but football is football in my eyes. Gaffney was not much bigger than where I was from, but it was a nice community and it was in close proximity to other big cities such as Charlotte, Greenville, and Spartanburg. This made the city more appealing than it was because you could drive to other cities and have fun. Once the security officer finished with the tour, he took us to Limestone's sporting complex. This is where we met all the coaches and got a chance for them to welcome us and give their disposition about the opportunity we were presented with and themselves as well. The complex was very nice. The locker rooms were huge, the walls were muraled with past players from different sports, the fields were maintained well, and the weight room was voted the nicest weight room in their conference. Limestone was known for their lacrosse programs because they were national champions almost every year or they made a deep playoff run. The athletic director was a cool guy and he welcomed us with open arms and anticipation. Once we saw the campus, met with the coaches, and I took my test, it was finally time to go. My family and I were exhausted from a long day of new experiences. This visit gave me two new ideas coming into my freshman year. I needed to make sure I stayed on top of my grades and I needed to work harder for this upcoming season because the competition looked tough.

Since I was going to be competing against some stiff competition, I decided I needed some help getting in the best playing shape possible. Working by myself was easy because I was self-motivated in everything I did, but I felt like I needed to reach another level to compete for playing time. There was only one person I could think of who could help me reach the level I needed to become better. When I was in fourth grade, I was able to meet a trainer who helped athletes and in general people with health goals. He was holding a weight loss competition at my school. I decided to enter the competition and I won. That competition allowed me to create a bond with him and he pushed me to be better. Unfortunately, we lost touch. However, I was able to find him again in a neighboring city where he had his own gym when I was in middle school. I worked with him for three years and I stopped once I was in high school. What better person to connect with being that I was going to play college football? Once I got in touch with him, I knew it was time to go to work.

"What we working for? When you get there, I don't want you to be just another player, I want you to make some noise. No need to train if you don't want to be a star." These are the words my trainer spoke to me religiously. He wanted me to be explosive and dominate as much as possible. He watched me grow into the football player I became and my success on the football field had a lot to do with him. He is one of the best trainers in the world and still trains athletes today. He pushed me beyond my limits relentlessly, day after day. Some days I didn't want to train, but I knew I had to get better. I worked five days a week until it was time for me to leave. Besides working out, preparing for my next chapter in football, I was spending time with my girlfriend and family.

My family supported me in everything I did. Every failure and every success they were there. My sister, Jasmine, and I were very close. We shared a special bond because we were both athletes. We worked out together and we pushed each other to be better daily. We were always in competition with each other. We would compete to see who drank water the fastest, who ran the fastest, even who could tie their shoe the fastest. Any time we could compete with one another we did. She helped my competitive edge grow and I always carried that around with me. My other sister's name is Shamyriah. She wasn't an athlete, but she was always supportive. We grew up dancing, fighting, laughing, and joking just like any other siblings. She was someone Jasmine and I grew closer to as we got older. I always have a feeling that something great is going to happen to her one day and I cannot wait to see it manifest. My father's name is Joseph. My father and I share a very unique bond. We have the same name, birthday, and I am his only son. I have lived with my father all my life and he was always the enforcer of the family. He worked hard to provide for us and never complained. He wasn't a big talker, but his presence always said it all. My father never missed a game I played in or an awards banquet I attended. He didn't play catch with me when I was younger, train me to get better, or gave me any criticism on my game. He didn't tell me he was proud of me until I was a senior in high school, and he didn't tell me he loved me until I was almost twenty-two. His actions showed us he loved us all. My father is the reason I went out and worked as hard as I did every day. Those are the morals and values he engraved in us as children. Work hard, don't complain, and take care of your family. My mother's name is Chematal or Pokey for those who cannot pronounce her real name.

My mother was the nurturer of the family. She kept the family solid. She always told me to give my best efforts no matter what. She celebrated my accomplishments with pride, but always made sure I remained humble and continued to work hard. She showered my sisters and I with unconditional love daily. Sometimes she was tough, but there was never a time we had to question her love for us. She never missed a game and always made sure to let me know if I played good or bad. These are the people I grew up with and who taught me how to grind and always work harder than the people you cannot see working.

My girlfriend's name was Jamellah. She was special to me. She was with me through all my success thus far and she supported me in everything I did. We got together when she was a sophomore and I was a junior in high school. We had our fair share of problems, but not once did she ever change her love or loyalty for me. She always drove me to work harder and grind for everything I wanted. We spent every day together until it was time for me to leave. She helped me pack my room up, made sure I had all the essential items I needed as well as things I wanted. While we were packing up my room, we were laughing and joking around. Out of nowhere, Jamellah burst out in tears. She began expressing a plethora of feelings and concerns she had about me leaving for school. She cried and we talked about our relationship and where we wanted to go. On that night, I made her a promise that we would make it and I would marry her one day. Yes, it was a big promise for a high school senior who was leaving her the next day. She knew I meant every word I said to her. As I wiped the tears from her face and her eyes, she looked me in my eyes with a look of happiness and safety. I wanted her to know I loved her, and I was with her for the long haul.

This was my last night in Bishopville and I didn't think I would be filled with mixed emotions. It was all becoming real. I was about to leave the people I have been with my entire life to be with a bunch of strangers for the next four years. The thought of leaving home was never a scary thought. The fact I was leaving behind the love and support that got me through all my years of school, sports, and life was the scary part. I spent as much time as I could with my family and my girlfriend that day. I knew when I woke up the next morning, this would no longer be my residence. I was leaving for the opportunity I dreamed of my entire life, but I didn't know if I was ready to leave behind my entire support system.

CHAPTER 3

Second and Six

The day has finally arrived for me to depart from my parents' home to my new home. My dreams were right in front of me and I was ecstatic. My family, my girlfriend, and I packed the cars and we headed down the road. I was eager and anxious about this new journey. When my family and I arrived on campus we had to finish the registration process. We walked to the gym and got in line to finish up the areas I did not complete during my summer visit. We went to various lines and once we were finished in the gym, we had to walk to the main building to receive my room key. My room was located in a building called New Dorms. There were four rooms in the suite and two beds per room. As I was moving my stuff in the room, my family and I met all of my roommates and their family. Everybody seemed pretty nice and I started to feel good about having multiple roommates.

My mom, girlfriend, and sister pretty much decorated my room and laid it out how they wanted. I was like an overseer the entire time. My roommate was a running back I played high school football with which made me feel a little more comfortable since I did not know anyone yet. He came in once we were done with my side of the room. As he was coming in, we were leaving to get cleaning supplies, bed décor, and food for my dorm. We took off to Walmart and began to shop for my supplies. As we were shopping, I received a text message from the coaches. It stated all players needed to report to the auditorium for the inaugural team meeting at 6:00 pm. I told them I had to go for the meeting, and everyone except my dad got teary-eyed and began to cry. I would have loved to spend more time with them but my priority at the moment was football.

I left Walmart and returned to school. I parked my car and walked to the auditorium for the meeting. This was all a new experience for me, and I was ready to learn as much as I could. I got in the auditorium and found a seat, eagerly waiting to meet the coaches. There were mannequins set up with game uniforms and a projector set up for the presentation by the coaches. The first coach who spoke to us was the head coach, Bobby James. This was his first head coaching job and he was full of enthusiasm and authenticity. The next coach was the defensive coordinator, Drew Anthony. This is the coach who recruited me. Coach Anthony was just as enthusiastic as Coach James and he showed it every day. The other coaches were my defensive line coach, offensive coordinator, and the offensive line coach. Each coach introduced themselves and gave a quick synopsis of their morals, values, and backstory. It was cool to meet new coaches who could help you grow as a player on this level. Once the meeting was adjourned, we were able to go back to our dorms and relax for the rest of the day. When I got back to my dorm my mom, girlfriend and sister had just finished getting my room together and putting things away. I was able to see them before they left which was a good feeling. I walked them outside to the car and gave them all my hugs and said my goodbyes. I was officially on my own and the people who had supported me all my life just left me.

I went back to my room and talked with my roommate for a while. We decided to go outside and walk around the campus. To our surprise, there was a group of players at a basketball court playing around and just introducing themselves to one another. I was pretty good at making friends and since we were going to be teammates, I might as well get to know everyone. I met the majority of the players that night. We laughed and joked for hours and finally decided to part ways, heading back to our dorms.

The next day we had to get ready for our weight lifting test and conditioning test. The coaches gave us a full day after registration to get rest and become prepared for the tests they were going to administer. When the time came, I was ready for whatever they were going to throw at us. We had to run the conditioning test early in the morning which was good for me. All of the linemen had to run a 40-yard shuttle. This meant we had to run 10 yards four times for each rep. The catch was we had to run fifteen of them and each one had to be done in ten seconds. I was never a die-hard for running, but I knew in order to play the game I love, I had to pass this first test. As we started running, it was by far the worst thing I have participated in my entire life. I failed on the ninth shuttle. I did not make it across the line in time. We all sat there until everyone finished their test. I felt terrible because I knew how hard I worked to prepare for the season. Not passing this test did not derail my spirits, but I was disappointed in myself. I had to work hard to redeem myself. The next test came later that day which was weightlifting. All players had to choose between 185lbs, 225lbs, 250lbs, 275lbs, and 315lbs. I was excited about this test because I worked out for years. When my turn came, I was ready to show and prove I was not a waste of their time. I was able to lift 315lbs fourteen times. I was happy about this, but I still knew I needed to pass the conditioning test as well. After both tests were completed for the day, the coaches called us in the weight room again to receive our equipment. The first official practice was the same afternoon as the day the tests were conducted. Once we were issued our equipment, we were to report to the locker room to get ready for practice. However, a few of the players along with myself were told to not get dressed. I didn't think much of it, but coach James came and talked to us privately. He simply told us we could not participate in the inaugural practice because we didn't pass the conditioning test early that morning. I felt even more terrible because I wasn't able to do what I came there to do. I wanted to play football and that process was interrupted due to a conditioning test. We had to sit at the practice field while our teammates went through a full practice without us. This was the first lesson

I learned at Limestone College. Coach James came to us after practice and said we all would get another try to pass the conditioning test the next morning with the players who were trying to walk on. There was no possible way I was going to fail again and let my dreams slip away from me.

It was a cool and breezy Wednesday morning. The test was scheduled at 9:00 am. I woke up out of bed and got dressed for the test. My mind and body felt different that morning. It was almost as if I was someone else. My roommate and I had to retake the test. We walked to the field and began to lace up our cleats so we could stretch. Just as the day before, the linemen were up first. Coach James blew the whistle and the test began. I knew I needed to pace myself better than I did the last time. I also knew I didn't want to fail this test again. When we got to the eighth shuttle, I was exhausted. The other players were on the sidelines, motivating us to stay strong and just keep pushing. We kept running and we finally made it to the final shuttle. Heavy breathing, legs burning, back hurting, sweat dripping, and dizziness were all the symptoms I was feeling at the time. I was in a zone and was prepared to do whatever I needed to do to finish strong on this last shuttle. When the whistle blew, I took off like I was being chased by a vicious dog. When I touched the line for the last turn and I knew I was going to make it, a feeling of joy came over me that I never experienced before. My college football dreams were finally about to become a reality. Later that afternoon, we had another practice and I was able to participate fully. This would be the first practice of many, and I was prepared to work my butt off to get a fair shot even though I was one day behind everyone else.

Our training camp lasted about two and a half weeks. I wasn't able to go home on the weekends and we worked daily from sunrise to sunset. We had two practices per day, multiple meetings throughout the day, and weightlifting. Football was the only thing we did every day until it was time for classes to start. When classes started, this was an entirely new world for me as well. I wasn't nervous about it because school came naturally to me. There was never a time growing up where I felt overwhelmed by school or nervous about failing a class. I was taking five classes in my first semester of college on top of playing football. My classes were fairly easy because they were all general education classes. I was majoring in mathematics to become a high school teacher. To be a college athlete, you must be committed and disciplined. You must be sure to prioritize and hold yourself accountable at all times. My daily schedule always seemed hectic. A normal day for me consisted of waking up at 6 am, showering, going to breakfast, attending to my first two classes, going to weightlifting, try to sneak something in for lunch, trying to make it to my next set of classes, going to defensive meetings, position meetings, getting ready for a 2-hour practice, leaving practice to make it to the cafeteria before they closed for the night, and trying to complete any assignments I had from class for the next day. I did this Monday through Thursday. On Fridays, my day started at 5:30 am because our defensive line coach wanted us at morning workouts by 5:45 am. Once our workout was done, my schedule resumed as Monday-Thursday minus the practice. Around the second month, while I was there, the football staff hired a new weightlifting coach for us. He stayed on top of us and pushed us because he wanted us to be better. He created weight programs and meal programs for every player on the team. On top of my already busy schedule, he talked to me privately about getting in some extra workouts during the week. I have never been one to back down from a challenge and I knew it could help me on the field. Somehow, I was able to squeeze these workouts into my schedule and he pushed me past my limits during every workout. Over the course of the fall semester, I learned so much from football and academically. The coaches were firm and fair. The professors and students were helpful as well. I wasn't much of a club or party-goer during my first year. I stayed in my dorm for the majority of the weekends I was there. On the weekends I wasn't there, I came home to spend time with my family and girlfriend. I stayed focused on my work and I stayed focused on the field. Every assignment, workout, meeting, practice, assessment, and obstacle I faced, I gave 100% at all times.

In the month of November, we were preparing to have a blue and white game for our parents and anyone else who wanted to attend. I felt like I played decently enough to get a good number of good snaps during the game. Everyone was going to get a chance to play because it was our first time in front of a crowd and the coaches wanted to see how everyone played. I played about six or eight plays during the game. I didn't get a tackle, but I changed a few outcomes on some plays. Once the game was over, I was able to meet with my family. My mom, dad, sisters, girlfriend, and Aunt Sharon came to the game. We went out to eat and celebrated the day. This game concluded the first player evaluation period and my first semester of college football was over. We still had to meet with the coaches one on one to discuss how the first semester went for us. I also had to finish strong with my classes.

The first coach I met with was my defensive line coach. This was an interesting meeting, to say the least. Me and him got along pretty well. The first thing he said to me in the meeting was, "I have to be honest Joe, I thought you were just another fat kid who was going to quit after the first week or two. You definitely proved me wrong and you are one of the players we are looking forward to coming back in the spring." I immediately began to laugh. As you all know by now, this has already happened before. I looked at him and told him, I was trained to be great, and quitting was never a word we could use in my house. He proceeded to talk with me about my grades, what I did well in, and how he thought I could improve for the spring. He told me I was seventh on the depth chart. This simply meant there were six players in the same position, who the coach's thought were better than me. I couldn't believe that because at no point did I see six players better than me. Once I finished meeting with him, I had to meet with Coach Anthony who was our defensive coordinator. Meeting with Coach Anthony was quick and simple. He pretty much told me my strengths and what he wanted me to improve on. He also expressed how they wanted me to play because of the strengths I had, and I could help us in the upcoming fall. After meeting with Coach Anthony, my last meeting was with Coach James. Coach James didn't mention much about football when I met with him. He talked more about my grades and life on the campus.

Overall, the meetings went well. I knew I had work to do over Christmas break if I wanted to improve my skills and make a statement in the spring. Every coach basically told me the fall didn't really matter. What you did in the spring would determine if you would get playing time in the upcoming season.

My first semester of college was officially over, and it was time to head home for winter break. I felt very accomplished because I passed all my classes and I was playing college football. I had high hopes for my second semester, and I knew it would be nothing short of amazing.

CHAPTER 4

Third and Three

School was back in session and I was moving back to Gaffney to start my second semester of college. I created my schedule for classes during the last semester and I was prepared to work extra hard this semester. I was only taking four classes this semester and I had my Tuesdays and Thursdays to myself. Football was a little different this semester because we couldn't practice with equipment on until March. From January until March, we had offseason conditioning. I have always hated conditioning, but I knew it was part of the game. Monday through Thursday, we would lift weights, have meetings, and have team conditioning. The conditioning usually lasted about an hour or so depending on how well we performed.

My classes for the semester were pretty easy and since I had two days of no classes, I was able to get a lot of work done. One of my professors during that semester asked us a question I had never really thought about. She asked us, "Where do you want to be in the next five years? In the next five years, you will all be adults and in the real world." This question scared me a little bit because I had never thought that far ahead. I especially never thought about life after football. This question stuck with me for a long time after she asked us. I started working extra hard when it came to football just in case, I got a chance to play at a higher level. Yes, I knew my chances were slim to play professionally but I still gave the game everything I had. The semester continued to pass by, and conditioning began to get a lot easier than it was in the beginning. When it was time for spring ball in March, I was ready to show off my new skills.

I was still seventh on the depth chart and that didn't sit well with me. I knew I had to have a good spring in order to move up. When we started practicing, every chance I got, I wanted to make a noticeable play. I felt like I should have been a rotation guy and I wanted to prove it every time I stepped on the field. I made plays the coaches probably thought I couldn't make. Spring practice was spread out through four weeks. Each week I moved up on the depth chart. One of our starting defensive tackles missed two and a half weeks of spring practice. During the time he was gone, I was working hard enough that I got promoted to the starting spot. I made tackles, batted down a pass or two, stopped screens, and never took a play off when I was on the field. We had our final practice a day before our spring game. The defensive tackle came back, and he was immediately given his role back.

I was feeling a little confused and I was a little pissed off. I was never a guy who worried about what others were doing because I knew as long as I controlled my actions and reactions everything would be fine. I busted my ass to get better and move up the depth chart. He only practiced one week the entire spring. All of a sudden, he comes back the day before the game and prepares to play as if he was there the entire time. The players thought it was wrong as well. Me being the person I am, I didn't say anything about the situation. I went out and played the game I loved as I normally would.

We played our spring game at the stadium we would be playing in the following year. It was named The Reservation. It was Gaffney High School's stadium. My family came up again to see me play in this game. My teammates and I played and competed against one another with passion and excitement. The game was over, and we went back to Limestone's campus. I met up with my family and my girlfriend after the game and we went to eat and enjoy each other's company. I told them about the situation that took place a few days before. They were just as upset as I was. The more I thought about the situation, the more I wanted to talk to my coaches about it. We had to meet with our coaches again before we left for summer break. I was eager to get in front of them because I wanted to know why the situation went down the way it did.

I met with my defensive line coach first. He welcomed me in, and I sat down with a clear mind and heart. As much as I thought about the situation and asking him why, I left the situation alone. I didn't want to bring up past events and I knew I played well all spring. He told me I graded out the highest on both sides out of every defensive tackle. He told me I played great during the spring and they were excited for me to play in the fall. He asked me what I felt I needed to work on and what my strengths were. I told him I needed to work on my speed and developing some pass rush moves. He agreed with me and told me I was guaranteed to be in the rotation of playing next season.

The next question I asked him, played a role in changing my entire perspective on college football and football in general. I was being awarded a $2,000 athletic stipend. I had good money from academic scholarships, but I still had to take out about $9,000 in student loans. Being that I played so well, I wanted to ask the coaches about receiving a little more money so I could lower my student loans. Before the meeting ended, I asked him, "Is there a possibility I could receive more scholarship money for the upcoming year." I didn't want them to cover all of my student loans, but I did feel like I earned another $1,000-$2,000. He told me, I should ask Coach Anthony or Coach James because that wasn't an answer, he could give me. I didn't think anything of it and I just said, "Ok sir I appreciate it." I walked out of the meeting feeling good, but I still had an uneasy feeling. My next meeting was with Coach Anthony. He was always excited for some reason. He welcomed me in, and I sat down to begin the meeting with him. He talked to me about my performance during the spring. He told me I had a unique skill set and I would definitely be playing in the upcoming season. He told me, he wanted me to stay the same weight and work on getting a little quicker. I was all in because again, this was my dream. Before the meeting adjourned, I asked him about an increase in my scholarship to help reduce my student loans. He told me I should ask Coach James because he is the one who distributes the funds. However, he also said, "You should definitely have that conversation with him because you had a hell of a spring and you deserve more money. If I were you, I would ask for more money as well." I left out of this meeting with a little more optimism than the first meeting. I told him I appreciated the meeting and I would be working hard this summer to be prepared for the next season. My last and final meeting came with Coach James. Coach James was a jokester and I felt like he was always honest and upfront with us. My meeting with him wasn't necessarily about football, but about life and a little football. He just wanted to make sure I was doing well, and everything was going well for me. We talked for about ten minutes before I asked him about the increase in scholarship money. From talking with other players as long as you had at least a 3.0 GPA and you were someone they were preparing to play the next season; you would get some type of increase in your scholarship. When I asked him about an increase, he told me he would have to check and see if there was any money left. He said he would get back with me and let me know once he checked. I simply said okay because again, I felt like coach James was a stand-up guy.

The offseason was over, and I was clear to focus on my academics. I stayed on top of my grades the previous semester and I was doing the same this semester. In the last week of classes, I received an email from the financial aid department. The email stated I was in jeopardy of losing my South Carolina Life Scholarship. This scholarship awarded me $5,000 per year. I was confused because I had a 3.0 GPA just like the requirements said I needed to have. What I didn't know at the time was I also needed 30 credit hours too. I immediately called financial aid and tried to find a solution to this problem because losing $5,000 was a big deal. They told me I would need to try and enroll in late spring classes and get the three hours I needed. My question to them was if they saw I needed the extra three hours, why they didn't contact me at the beginning of the semester. I didn't have a class on Tuesday or Thursday. I was upset about that because losing this scholarship would mean I needed to take out more student loans. Luckily, I was able to get in a class during late spring enrollment.

I was outside of the dorms walking around the campus thinking about this situation and I saw CJ sitting in front of his dorm. He was one of the defensive linemen on the team. I walked up and began talking to him about what happened to me. The funny thing is, the exact same thing happened to him. We both started laughing and joking about the situation. That conversation was the start of our friendship. We became friends from that day forward and we still are until this day. I talked with him for a while longer and eventually went back to my dorm. I had to find a class during this late spring enrollment. I looked through the academic catalog to find a class that would be suitable for me. The class I signed up for was public speaking. I didn't know how this class would go because I assumed you needed to be physically in a class to take public speaking, but I was fortunate to get into this class.

The class would run from May until June. I was completely out of school mode even though I needed this class to keep my scholarship. I didn't complete any assignments during this class. I didn't buy the book I needed or interact with the students and professor. I literally sat home and did no work. Like most students try and do when it came to the end of the class, I was asking the professor a million questions to help me improve my grade. I did nothing productive the entire duration of this class, but I wanted her to help me improve my grade. I needed to make at least a C in the class to keep my 3.0 GPA and my scholarship. The worst part of the whole situation was, my parents had to pay out of pocket for me to take this class. If I didn't pass, it would have been a slap in the face to them. I begged and begged her to let me do some extra work or retake the assessments. She actually gave me an opportunity to retake the assessments that were given earlier in the class. There was a total of four assessments I needed to take and pass. Every test I took, I failed. I used Google, Quizlet, and every other resource I could find to help me pass these tests. I still failed every one of them. The professor was gracious enough to give me a D as a final grade. I remember thinking to myself, how am I going to tell my parents about this class. I remember my mom looking me in my eyes and saying, "I know damn well you ain't waste my money and fail this class?" What could I say to make this situation make sense? I was lazy, unmotivated, and wasted my parent's money. Throughout this entire process, I had also been hired for my first job. I was a cashier at Walmart for the entire summer. Here I was trying to take a class for my scholarship and working to possibly repay my parents for the lack of commitment and discipline I showed.

I learned some valuable lessons while working just as I did at Limestone. I learned to work hard, mind your business, don't believe everyone who smiles in your face, and the world is filled with ignorant people. I got into a verbal altercation that almost ended up being a physical altercation with an older Caucasian man. This altercation taught me a valuable lesson about people in the world and Coach James was 100% right. The only thing you can do is control what you can control. The older white man came to my register and after I was done bagging his items, I mistakenly forgot to give him his change. We had to wait for a manager to come over and open the register again, which took about 30 seconds. In that 30 second window, he called me a stupid cashier and said he wanted his money back. I immediately flipped and began to say some things I probably shouldn't have said at the time. My manager came over and told me to go sit in customer service to calm down, but I was fine. I went in customer service and the man came in and was still talking crazily. I simply told him, "Speak to me directly unless you want to get slapped today. In the moment, I didn't care what happened because I felt disrespected. I was young and ignorant of the world even though I was somewhat exposed on my first visit at Limestone.

I should have handled the situation differently, but again I was young and immature in a sense. This situation blew over and now I had to figure out how I would make up for the scholarship I lost. I had 30 credit hours, but I ended up with a 2.9 GPA for the year. I thought about all possible scenarios and I remembered I was supposed to contact Coach James about possibly receiving more scholarship money. I needed it now more than ever. When I contacted him and asked about the extra money, he told me there was no money left. This news was definitely disappointing, but I had to accept it. After spending two or three days in deep thought, I decided I would have to go to a different school. I couldn't afford to stay at Limestone since I lost my scholarship and I wasn't getting extra money from football. Not receiving any money was also when I realized how much of a business college football was. I contacted my defensive line coach and Coach Anthony out of respect to let them know I wouldn't be coming back. When I sent these messages, Coach Anthony called me immediately. He asked me what was going on and why wasn't I coming back. I basically told him I couldn't afford to come back because of the situation I was in. He told me not to worry just yet, but he would get back to me later that day or the next day. My defensive line coach didn't say much and neither did Coach James. It was cool with me because I didn't know if I wanted to continue playing football after that year anyway. Being at Limestone made me contemplate leaving the game I love, and I didn't want to play like that. I spent the rest of my summer looking for a new school I could attend and possibly play football again.

CHAPTER 5

Fourth and Inches

My love for football slowly went away once I realized how much business played into it. I knew I wasn't a top recruit, but I felt I played well enough to get a few extra dollars for the next school term. In the words of Coach James, control what you can control. I looked at many different schools. I knew if I wanted to play football again, I needed to go somewhere I would have an opportunity. Coach Anthony couldn't do anything for me, and he apologized for not being able to help me. He did what he could, and I was appreciative of that. I looked around for about a week, trying to find a school to enroll in during the fall. I eventually decided to enroll at Benedict College. My cousin was going there at the time and she was telling me I should come there. My girlfriend was also about to start college. She talked to me about possibly coming with her. She was going to Claflin, but they didn't have a football team. I filled out the application for Benedict College, sent my transcript from high school and Limestone, and awaited a response.

Within three days I received a letter saying I was accepted. I was excited because I felt like I could leave Limestone behind me and start fresh. I went to Benedict to get registered for my classes, receive my schedule, room assignment, and possibly talk with the football coach about walking on. I completed the entire registration process. I received my schedule, and I was waiting to see what dorm room I would be in. I went to the restroom for a moment before they called my name. As I walked out and looked around, something told me I shouldn't be here. I'm not sure where the thought came from but being there at that moment did not feel right.

I went outside the building to call Limestone. I knew I owed them a balance from the late spring class I took, but time was winding down and they were familiar for me. The problem was I didn't know if I would have to pay to attend school for the year. I lost my LIFE scholarship and I didn't get any extra money from the athletic department. Therefore, I was a little skeptical about returning.

When I called them, I spoke with someone in financial aid about returning to the school. I also talked with them about the money I needed to pay before I could return. The lady told me I only owed them $260. I was lucky to have the money to pay myself since I worked the entire summer. I was fortunate I didn't have to ask my parents. Once I got home, I explained the situation to them and let them know I would be attending Limestone again. Once I knew I was going back to Limestone, I contacted Coach James, Coach Anthony, and my defensive line coach. I knew I wanted to play football again and being that I was going back to Limestone, I felt like I had a chance to get back on the team. They were all excited to hear from me and welcomed me back with open arms. I was excited to get back on the field with some of the players I recently played with and the new players that were recruited. I knew things wouldn't be like they were before I left because they didn't account for me being there. I packed my bags once again so I could head to Gaffney for a second year.

When I got to school, I went to the admissions office to get my paperwork squared away. Once I was done with admissions, I was assigned to my new room in an apartment complex called Chandler Oaks. I was sharing a room with two football players from last year's recruits. I was also right across the yard from CJ and some other teammates from the previous year. I was excited to be back and see what this year had in store for me. As my parents and I were moving my stuff in the apartment, my roommates walked in. I was roommates with CJ's cousin OC and a player we called Bluff. They were already good friends and had both of the rooms to themselves. I did not want to intrude and move things around, I just put my bed in the living room and made it my personal room. My parents moved me in, made sure I had groceries, money in my pocket, and wished me well. They left me there without thought which was fine by me, I was ready to take on this second year by storm.

I settled in my apartment and soaked in the moment. I was really back at Limestone for another year. The football players were just getting out of practice as I was settling and everyone from last year's team welcomed me back as if I never left. We laughed, joked, and talked for a while. They were telling me about the new players, coaches, and what to expect when I got back to the field. I wasn't worried because I always felt like football was football no matter who or where I played. Once we finished talking, the players went to their apartments and I sat in my apartment talking to OC and Bluff about the apartment and us living together. We became pretty good friends that year and we are still cool with one another today.

The next day came and I needed to talk with Coach James and my defensive line coach. I went to the coach's office and met all the coaches. They were excited to see me and asked me different questions about my summer, how I felt, and if I was ready to get back on the field. Of course, I was ready! I wanted to play football no matter what. I had not done much working out over the summer and I knew being in shape was going to be a priority if I wanted to compete at a high level. They told me I needed to pass the conditioning test in order to start practicing. I understood that and my mind was already trained to push through and get back on the field. I went to practice that same day and watched everyone to get a feel for the practice environment. There were a few players who still had to take the conditioning test who watched practice with me. We all sat and introduced ourselves to one another while we became acquainted. As I was sitting there talking with the players, the weightlifting coach walked by us. He stopped and greeted me with a big smile. He asked if was I going to play again. I told him yes,

I just had to take the conditioning test tomorrow. He told me congratulations and he could not wait to see me back in the weight room. I continued to watch practice and when it was over, I went to grab some food with a few teammates. This was my first real interaction with the football team, I was eagerly prepared for the next interaction.

The next day came and I was prepared to take the conditioning test. The assistant defensive line coach was giving me the test. I didn't know him, but he seemed like a pretty straight forward guy. I was scheduled to run the test right before the players came out for practice. I got to the field, stretched my legs, and was ready to run. I knew it would be challenging, but I was ready to push myself to my limits to pass this test. The coach blew the whistle and I began the test. Once I got to the third shuttle, a few of the players who were my close friends began to come out and motivate me while I was running. I was doing decent, but I was getting tired. When I got to number seven, the head defensive line coach came out to the field as well because practice was about to begin. I had to make each shuttle in 10 seconds or less. Once I got to the seventh shuttle, I was crossing the line between nine and ten seconds. When I got to the eighth shuttle, I crossed the line just in time. The head defensive line coach told me if I made the time that close again, he wasn't going to let me finish the test. I didn't pay it any attention because I was beating the time. As he was talking, Bluff was also telling me not to pay attention to what he was saying, just keep doing what I was doing. On the ninth shuttle, as my entire body crossed the line, he told me the test was over, to try again another day. All the players were looking confused and didn't understand why he failed me. When he stopped the test, I honestly wanted to slap him. I knew I crossed the line in time and so did everyone standing there but what could I do in that moment? I was not on the team. I was just like any other player trying out even though I played the year before. The players tried to pep me up, but I was pissed, and the defensive line coach knew I was.

I stayed and watched the team practice once again. I took the next day to prepare myself for the test again. The assistant defensive line coach offered me another chance to take it. Two days later, I was back at the field ready to try again. The defensive line coach told me if I didn't pass this time, I shouldn't come back. I was ready to start it and get it over with. He blew the whistle and I began the test. When I got to the tenth shuttle, I was beyond tired. I didn't know how I was going to make it through the last five. I pushed through the eleventh shuttle, but on the twelfth shuttle, I didn't make the time. He told me because I was working so hard, he was going to let that one slide. My friends were out there talking trash and pushing me once again. They were trying to give me water, forcing me to stay up and pushing me non-stop to finish the last three. When I got to the fifteenth shuttle and crossed the line, I immediately fell to the ground from exhaustion. The coach told me if I did not get off the ground and stand up in the next three seconds, he would fail me. I immediately hopped off the ground and stood there. He came to me and told me, the only reason he passed me was because I seemed like a hard-working kid and he knew sitting out would do more harm than good. He also finished by saying I shouldn't make him regret his decision. I was fortunate for the opportunity and I definitely was not about to waste it. All my friends were excited I was back in action and the other coaches seemed happy as well. I was ready for the next phase of my football journey.

Being back on the team was a great feeling and I knew I would have to work my way up on the depth chart again. The first year, we didn't play any games which made the season awkward. This season was a lot different compared to last season. The team was basically split into two teams. There was the travel squad which were the players that always dressed for games and there was the practice squad or scout team. I was placed on the practice team once I passed the conditioning test. I was fine with that because I knew I could make the travel team. When I got my equipment, I was excited and ready to start practicing. The thing that caught me off guard was, the scout team had to be up at 6:00 am every Tuesday morning to go over the practice plan we would be trying to execute for the week. I honestly hated these meetings because I thought they were pointless. We stayed in the meetings for about an hour and we went back to our dorms to get some sleep before classes. When I got to my first official practice and met the scout team players, I officially introduced myself to everyone. Once I introduced myself to the players, I huddled all the defensive linemen and told them, "I know we are supposed to rotate every three or four plays, but I'm not rotating with nobody." I told them they could rotate with the other defensive tackle and when I was ready to come out, I would let somebody else get reps. Yea, it was an asshole move, but I needed to get in football shape and get back to the level of football I knew I was capable of playing.

Being on the practice squad was fun for me. I had a chance to practice against the starting offensive lineman every day. Some of them were good and others not so good. What better way to prove to the coaches I was able to play than to make plays against the starting offensive lineman? As much I was ready to play football, some days I didn't feel like practicing. However, my motto was even though I don't want to be here, I'm here now. I might as well make somebody feel uncomfortable while I'm here. There were days I practiced really well and other days where I practiced hard enough. I talked trash to the players and the coaches just to make practice fun. My favorite guys on the practice squad was a linebacker named Blair, defensive end named Chris, and a defensive tackle named Tre. All of us made our presence known every day. I practiced for two weeks on the practice squad and I was getting the hang of the morning meetings and what the coaches expected from us. When the third week of practice came, I went hard all week and on Thursday, the defensive line coach pulled me aside right before practice started. He told me the offensive coaches said I was practicing very well. They wanted to put me on the travel squad the week before, but he said I didn't practice hard enough the previous Thursday and that is why they did not bring me with them. He told me to go out and have a good practice and I would be traveling with them Saturday. That was an easy task, I just had to go out and do what I normally do in practice. After practice was over, sure enough, he told me I would be promoted to the travel squad.

Being promoted to the travel seemed like it would be a great situation to be in. However, I honestly wish I would have stayed with the scout team. I was very fortunate for the opportunity because I got a chance to travel to Kentucky and Florida for the first time in my life. That was the only exciting thing about moving to the travel squad. I sat on the sidelines in practice and at games. All I did was look in the crowd and made sure players had water. My first official play in a college football game, I forced a QB hurry. I made a few other plays, but it was nothing to celebrate. I was pissed for the remainder of the year I spent on the travel squad. My mindset has always been realistic and optimistic. I knew I was good enough to play two or three plays per quarter in a game, but the coaches did not see me in that capacity. I played a total of fifteen plays my entire college career. As the last game was approaching, I made my mind up I was done playing football. I busted my ass for two years and all I got to show for it was fifteen plays.

My homeboy CJ and I made our minds up we weren't going back for spring ball. I was disappointed I didn't get a chance to play as much, but I also understood the business aspect of the game. I knew after the experiences I had from those two seasons, I did not want to be a part of the business. I was prepared to walk away from the game without remorse or conflicted feelings. When the season came to an end, I turned in my equipment and was content with my decision. I knew that would be the last time I put on football equipment and I was okay with that decision. Some people may say I gave up on my dream, but I didn't give up at all. I made a decision based on the outside forces of football. Money ran the football world and I knew I would not sacrifice my body daily without receiving adequate compensation for my worth. I finished the semester strong and prepared myself for Christmas break. I had not seen my girlfriend or my family in four months because of the season. I was pretty eager to see them and let them know my decision. This semester was definitely a lesson learned and I took it with me as fuel for the rest of my life.

CHAPTER 6

Punt

Once I got home for Christmas break, I didn't want to rush into my decision. I was happy to see everyone, and it felt good to be home for a break. After being home for a few days, I finally decided to tell my parents and my girlfriend about my decision. We all sat around in my living room talking and I told them I had an announcement to make. When I revealed I wasn't going to play football anymore, they were a little shocked by the news. Of course, questions came next. What happened? When did you decide this? Are you sure? Are you going to try and go somewhere else to play? What are you going to do now? I was prepared to answer all of these questions because I made my decision long before the season was over. I explained how the business aspect of football was something I didn't want to be part of. I also explained how upset I was with the season. I felt like the amount of playing time I received was a slap in the face after all the work I put in to be part of the program. I had no intention of participating in spring ball during the offseason. I knew that would make my football career come to an official end.

This conversation continued for about another hour. I answered all the questions they asked me with solid answers except what my next move was. I didn't want to think about that decision over my break. I wanted to enjoy being away from school, my family, and friends. Since I didn't have to work out or stay in football shape, I had a great break with my family and friends. We went out, played games, had cookouts, and the holidays were great as well. My time home began to decrease, and I started to have thoughts about my life without football. This is the game I have been playing since I was a young kid at Lee County Parks and Recreation. What was I going to do now that football was in my rearview?

I packed my bags again and got ready to go back to Limestone for the second semester. My parents took me back to Gaffney and I prepared for the semester. Classes started the next day and I was enjoying my new schedule. The only problem was, I was done every day by 11:00 am or 12:00 pm. Normally, I would be preparing for meetings, weightlifting, or practice. I was definitely not use to having this much time on my hands. I had time like Jeff Bezos has money. I needed to find a hobby because if not, I probably wouldn't have done well in my classes. CJ and I were always together during the second semester. He is part of the reason I continued to go to class and do what I was supposed to do. Our daily interactions helped me stay positive and continue to do my work even when I didn't feel like doing anything. It wasn't that he was my best friend, but it had more to do with the fact that we were two of the only players recruited the year before who didn't play anymore. We shared the same mindset about the team and we both didn't want to fail now that football wasn't in the picture. All the guys I was friends with were handling their business. Being that I was associated with them I didn't want to be the failure of the group by not handling my business. Having positive energy from other friends who still played football also helped me push myself when I didn't want to handle my business. The only thing I knew was I didn't want to be left behind when all my friends moved on to get degrees.

As the semester continued, I started utilizing my time more efficiently. Whether I was doing assignments ahead of time, playing games, or doing research to figure out my next plan of action, my time was being used in the best way possible. This was the first time in 10-12 years I had not been associated with football. A lot of players asked me if I missed it. Some told me I probably didn't miss it now, but I would in a few months. The number one question I was always asked was, why did I give it up? Honestly, the coaches were fickle. They wanted me to give them my full worth, but only gave me ten percent of my worth. Yes, I know college football is a business, but there is no way I was going to give a full commitment to a group of men who couldn't even be honest with me. Some people may say I went about the situation the wrong way. Some may say I was being selfish and felt a sense of entitlement. There are many opinions that can form when you're on the outside looking in. I understand everyone has their own opinion and may have used different methods in this situation. I knew I personally didn't want to put myself in a situation where I had to commit to a team that wouldn't commit to helping me. I have no resentment towards any of the coaches or how they handled their business. I sent all of them a thank you message because if it had not been for them recruiting me, I would not have had the opportunities I had then and have now. I would not have met my brothers and developed lifelong bonds with teammates. I would not have created bonds with some of the coaches. I would not have been as serious about going to college. I would not have been able to grow and fight through adversity as I am able to today. Therefore, I thank them for how they helped changed my life, but I knew it was time for me to move on from this chapter in my life. The semester was coming to a close and I was in the process of finalizing my plan and putting it into action.

I was able to finish the year with a 2.94 GPA. I was content with that and since I lost my scholarship during the summer, it wasn't a big deal to me. During the last week of the semester, I told my friends I wouldn't be coming back to Limestone. They tried to convince me I should stay, but I wasn't playing football anymore and my student loans were already too high for my liking. I ordered a few transcripts and sent them to different schools. I sent my transcripts to Coastal Carolina University, Francis Marion University, Savannah State University, and Coker College. I wanted to keep my options open and didn't want to condemn myself to one university in the event I didn't get accepted. I completed the admission application for these schools and awaited a response from them. In the midst of finding a new school, I needed to find a job for the summer. Luckily, my aunt's job was doing a summer program for college students. She gave me the application for the job and once I completed it, she gave it to her manager. My first job was the summer after my first year of college at Walmart. This job was completely different from working at Walmart. Working at this industrial plant is the reason I vowed I would stay in school and graduate. I commend everyone who works in plant jobs because they are special individuals. I was employed at this job for three weeks before the program had to be terminated due to budget cuts in their corporation. I wasn't even mad we had to lose the job. I was back home with no job and still trying to make the best decision I could for school. I weighed the pros and cons of every school before I made a final decision. Ultimately, it came down to who was the cheapest and student to teacher ratio. Limestone had small classes and it was easier to receive help and interact with professors and classmates. I never wanted to attend a big university where I would be just a number. I wanted a more intimate setting where I could ask questions and actually learn the material. There was one school from my list that stuck out from the others, Francis Marion University. They were cost-efficient and they were a prestigious university known for their academics. Once I knew this was the university I wanted to attend, instead of sending the paperwork in, I hand-delivered the paperwork to their office. I will discuss that process in later chapters.

Now that I had figured out the school I wanted to attend, I needed to find a job until it was time for me to enroll in August. I put in applications every day, but it seemed like I had no luck. Eventually, I received a phone call for an interview at Kohl's. Kohl's is a major department store. I did very well in the interview, and they offered me the position. I was grateful for the position because I had another chance to make some money before I started school. I enjoyed this job, but it was just another stepping stone until I could get back in school. Aside from working for the remainder of the summer, I also spent time with my family and girlfriend. This was a very different summer for me because I wasn't getting prepared to play football anywhere. All summer I was faced with questions and backlash about my decision to walk away from football. No one understood my position and I didn't explain it to them. I wasn't missing the game like people said I would, and I wasn't itching to go back and play. This was the first time in my life I had a free summer to do whatever I pleased without worrying about the consequences. The second semester I spent at Limestone spoiled me with having extra time on my hands. Playing football was honestly the last thing on my mind. I started to fall in love with the thought of having free time and doing what I wanted. I didn't have to worry about meetings, practices, scheduled workouts, or leaving home early to go to camp. It was a great feeling to be free, but the summer was passing by pretty quickly. I was having so much fun spending time with my girlfriend and family, I almost forgot I didn't finish up some important decisions I needed to make before August came.

As August was approaching, I began to do more research on Francis Marion and figure out when I would go see the campus and take care of the necessary paperwork. I continued working at Kohl's, but I didn't want to continue working while going to school as well. I gave them a two weeks' notice to inform them I wouldn't be returning. After my final day working, I knew I still needed to go to Francis Marion to get my paperwork squared away. I didn't know what to expect going to a new school. I was leaving all my friends behind and starting my college journey over. There were a few of my classmates and high school peers enrolled in Francis Marion as well, but I didn't talk with many people from high school. Going to Francis Marion would be the start of a new journey in my life and I was ready to start this adventure in a new environment. It would give me a chance to network with new people, learn new lessons, and see if I could push myself without my friends and without football as a motivating outlier.

CHAPTER 7

Forced Fumble

Going to a new environment is never easy for anyone. Change is one of the scariest monsters of life. If you aren't prepared for it, you could become overwhelmed when it comes. I was preparing for this moment for months now and I was prepared to face whatever came my way. As mentioned earlier I wanted to hand-deliver the necessary paperwork to Francis Marion. This would give me a chance to see the campus and meet new people. My mother, sister, and I headed to Francis Marion to hopefully return home with good news. When I got to the campus, I had to go to the office of admissions. Everyone we came in contact with was nice and friendly. They helped me with any questions or concerns I had. My mother and I sat in the admissions office while the admission clerks looked over my transcript. One of them asked me what my GPA was from my previous school and did I know what I wanted to major in. When I left Limestone, I was majoring in mathematics and that is what I wanted to stick with. I explained to them I lost my LIFE Scholarship due to unknown requirements I did not meet, and I was hoping there was a way I could receive it again by attending this university. She told me I needed to have 60 credit hours and a 3.0 GPA to reapply for the scholarship as a sophomore. Unfortunately, I didn't meet either of these requirements. She said I could receive it if I could finish my junior year with 90 credits and a 3.0 GPA. That was an impossible task seeing as I only had 48 credit hours. Although I couldn't get the LIFE scholarship back, she did tell me I was eligible to receive the South Carolina Tuition Grant. This grant wasn't as much as the LIFE Scholarship, but it would help lower my student loans. While we were discussing my financial needs, the other admissions clerk was comparing my classes from Limestone to the curriculum at Francis Marion to see how many of my classes would transfer to their university. I was confused about what that meant. Nobody told me when you transfer from one university to another, there is a chance your previous classes won't transfer with you. When she said that, all the enthusiasm left my body. If my classes didn't transfer, I would have to start my collegiate journey from scratch. All the work I put in at Limestone would basically be erased. All I could do was wait in suspense and hope all my classes transferred.

Finally, she came with good news, I was beyond excited when she told me all my classes would transfer. On top of all my classes transferring, my GPA would start over which basically gave me a clean slate. After all the paperwork was done in admissions, she told me I needed to go by the financial aid department to make sure my finances were taken care of for the year. She also mentioned I needed to come back the next day for orientation. I thanked them for their assistance, and we walked to the financial aid department. I wasn't there long, and I was able to receive the funds I needed to attend school all while getting a refund as well. The school was cheap for me because I was going to commute. I didn't want to stay on campus with new people after I left Limestone. I was beginning to like this school more and more. I left the campus eager and anxious for the next day.

My mother and I woke up the following morning and headed to Francis Marion for orientation. When we got there, orientation had already begun. We walked to the auditorium and sat there for what seemed to be an eternity. They talked about the campus, the major accomplishments of the university, and some students talked about their experiences. Once they finished talking, the students were broken into groups according to their majors. There weren't many students majoring in math, but I was excited to meet new people. We toured the campus, met the staff in the math department, received our schedules, catalogs, and a schedule of the classes we would need to take to graduate on time. The orientation was for freshman, but since I was a new student, I had to attend. After getting all the information I needed from orientation, my mother and I left. Classes started in a week and I was eager to start. I'm not sure what made me so excited, but I wish that enthusiasm stayed with me.

Classes started on a Tuesday afternoon, but I didn't have to go until Wednesday. I prepared my mind all weekend to start this new journey. My first day of classes went well, the campus was easy to get around, the class sizes were perfect, the professors were great as well. Overall, it was just an all-around great first day. I was hopeful the next day would be the same since I had to attend different classes. I woke up bright-eyed and bushy-tailed, washed, put my clothes on, and drove to school. I got to my class and waited for my day to start. I met a new set of professors and a new set of students in each class. By the end of the day, I was extremely optimistic I chose the perfect university. As most schools follow the same protocol, the first few days were for introductions, campus academic policies, and the rules and procedures personalized by the professors. The rules were simple, fair, and easy enough to follow. After my first week, I was sure Francis Marion gave me everything I wanted in a school to keep me motivated without having football. At least that was my thought at the time.

My first few weeks at Francis Marion were great. I learned new skills, met new people, and was adjusting to life without football. Since I was majoring in math, I had to start from the beginning of their math program. The first class in their program was Calculus 1. I have been good with numbers all my life. I wasn't worried about passing the calculus class because of my prior knowledge and history with math classes. Although I was good with numbers, I hadn't taken a math class since I was a senior in high school, which was three years prior. I didn't think that mattered much, but man was I wrong. Calculus was like taking a foreign language class. The professor we had was amazing. She was very knowledgeable and willing to help the students as much as she could. I felt like I was learning the material and confident I was going to do well on our upcoming exam. However, when I got the test in front of me, I was completely lost. I didn't know the first step to use when trying to complete the problems. Before I finished the test, I knew I was going to fail. Sure enough, when I got my test back, I got an F. I was doing well in my other classes. I passed all the assignments and exams in those classes. Calculus was a different story. The one skill I never learned in high school was how to properly study outside of class. Yes, I could review the information and retain it for future use. However, calculus was a class that required you to really put time and effort into it. On top of struggling to pass this class, I started working to make some extra money. I was working at Walmart and trying to improve my grades in my calculus class.

After I received my first F, things began to go downhill. I started going to class late which could cause me to fail. I didn't study for exams and I was developing habits I never had before. If a student was late three times, the professor would equate that to one absence. If a student reached six absences, they would automatically receive an F for the course. Every day, I started testing the water with time seeing how late I could leave home and make it to school. I'm not sure why I did it, but I was late every day for this class except for about eight classes. I was being late so much, my professor started locking the door if we weren't on time. There were sometimes I was late and had to sit on the outside of the class while looking through the door as she taught the class. Once class was over, I would go in the classroom and ask a question to let her know I was outside the door trying to pay attention. Once I got my second F on an exam, I just gave up on the class. I didn't take the class seriously anymore and I was just going through the motion of being there. I failed every exam I took in this class. Of course, my overall grade was an F as well. This was the first time in my life I got an F in any class. Most people would probably stress and become overwhelmed with the results I received. However, I am an optimistic person in all situations no matter how bad they may seem.

Once I knew I failed the class, I had to sign up for the class again. The math director, who was also my academic advisor, told me I needed to pass Calculus 1 before I could double up on math classes. The longer I took to pass calculus, the longer I would have to stay in school. My advisor and I made my schedule and I enrolled in the same calculus class with the same professor. I knew what to expect this time and I was more confident than before. I felt like the material I was able to store in my working memory was going to play to my advantage while taking the class a second time around. Once the first semester came to an end, I spent my Christmas break working and thinking about how to change the bad habits I developed to be successful in the spring semester. I was taking the same professor at the same time. The first semester, calculus beat me like when I cursed at my parents. I was not going to take that lightly. I was coming back for revenge during the second semester.

My first semester was a great one, minus the F. However, my second semester was not one to remember. The spring semester of 2016 was the start of me having to figure out my life and who I was. From the months of January to May, I bought my first car, got fired from Walmart (on my day off), failed calculus again, and was starting to miss football. When the first day of classes came, I was the first student there. It was important to me that I made a statement during the first week or two. I started the semester strong. I was getting to class early, going to help sessions, asking questions to gain understanding, and studying when I got home. There was no way possible I was going to repeat what I did the first semester. A few weeks passed, and I was excited because I thought I was getting the hang of the instruction. Let's just say, my first exam grade slapped me in my face like a hurricane wind. I looked at that F and was in complete shock. I knew I was doing better, taking things more seriously, and utilizing my time the best way I could. Clearly, calculus didn't care about any of that because it was still laughing at me as if I were a comedian. Once again, I was back at square one. The first F led to a series of Fs. I did well enough to pass my other classes and calculus beat me like it was Mike Tyson. There was no possible way I ever imagined failing the same class twice. I was at Francis Marion for two semesters and I had already failed two classes. Along with failing calculus again, I was also trying to make my way back into the football world and find a new job to make my car payment. Yes, I know my plate was full, but I was working every day to reach my desired goals. I didn't want to go back and play football, but I knew I wanted to be around the sport. Throughout the spring semester, I looked for coaching jobs throughout the state. Hopefully getting a coaching job would eliminate my hunger for football and my financial issues. I sent multiple emails and resumes to different coaches. I didn't care where I ended up, I just knew I wanted an opportunity to be around the game again. I was still trying to find a part-time job to cover my car payment and insurance as well. My thoughts were all over the place. I wasn't passing calculus, I was going through a financial transition, and I was missing football which was the one thing that kept me balanced and motivated. My girlfriend was still in college as well and she was always fussing at me about not doing my best and I needed to get it together. It was like I was in an alternate reality. Unlike Limestone, I didn't have any friends around me to motivate me to be better. When I drove to the campus, I went to my classes, listened to music, watched Netflix in between classes, and once class was over, I got in my car to go home. There was never a time I stayed on campus to converse with anyone or held a conversation over five minutes with anyone. I didn't even know where the cafeteria was located on the campus. I needed to find a way to get back to myself.

After sending numerous emails and resumes without getting any feedback, I decided to go to my old high school and check out the football team. I sent the head coach an email a day or two before

I went to the school. When I got there, the kids were lifting weights. They didn't do very well the season before, but that was understandable because the coaches were new, and they came in very late. I knew two of the coaches on the staff because they coached me in high school. I introduced myself to the head coach while I was there. His name is Justin Danner. He also introduced me to Lester Davis, who was the assistant head coach and the defensive coordinator. Coach Danner and I never interacted with one another before this time, but the conversation was interesting. As a player, you don't really pay attention to a lot of things outside of playing, but Danner actually coached against me while I was in high school. I won't bring up records but let's just say those aren't moments I want to relive. We talked for a while and I gave him my information for a later date. I felt good leaving the school because I thought we had a good conversation and I could have an opportunity to get where I wanted to be.

I was fortunate to receive a phone call from him a few days later and he offered me a position helping my old defensive line coach. I was excited because football was going to be a part of my life again and I received a job opportunity. Having this job opportunity was a great feeling, but I still had to deal with school which wasn't my best friend at the moment. My girlfriend was excited for me because she knew how much I was struggling. Spring football was coming up and this was my first-time coaching. I was a little nervous, but I was excited to be part of this life again. A week or so before spring ball started, Coach Danner called me to inform me I would be changing positions. Instead of working as an assistant defensive line coach, he needed me to be the new offensive line coach. I was a little shocked because I didn't have any coaching experience and he was giving me an entire group to maintain and control by myself. Although I was surprised, I was prepared to take on this role because I loved football.

Now that I had a coaching position, I thought it would solve my financial problems as well. That idea got dropped immediately. High school coaches get paid at the end of their seasons. Therefore, I was still in a financial struggle trying to make a car payment and car insurance. I was also in the process of trying to get over a rough school year. I made it out of my first year at Francis Marion with a few scars, but it made me stronger. Now that I was back around football, I was happy again and my girlfriend was on my case daily about doing better. Everything was beginning to make sense once again. Once school was out, my entire summer was dedicated to learning the game of football as a coach and figuring out my place on the field without playing. I didn't worry much about school at the beginning of the summer because I was trying to put that whole year behind me and start fresh in August. I learned a lot over the summer about coaching from Coach Danner. He took me under his wing and developed me into the coach I am today. As August approached quickly, I had to program my mind to focus on school again. Although my first year wasn't great, I was back around football and I knew in order to be the coach I wanted to be, I needed to do well and get out of school. My mindset was 100% focused on being the student I knew I was capable of being during my second year. The reality of my second year was dropping out or possibly getting kicked out.

CHAPTER 8

Interception

My second year at Francis Marion was by far my worst year of school and the lowest I felt in my life. There were multiple factors that played into these feelings and the way I handled situations. The only shining light I had was my girlfriend, Jamellah and football. As the school year was approaching, I already locked my mind on making As and Bs only. I knew I was more than capable of achieving the grades I wanted. It was just a matter of if I was going to do what was necessary to get the results I wanted. I was still trying to survive financially to keep my car and have money in my pocket. We always received our refund the week before we started classes. When I registered for Francis Marion and received my financial aid, they gave me the South Carolina Tuition Grant as I stated. Due to those two Fs I received, I lost that scholarship as well. I was only receiving a Pell grant and student loans to fund my schooling. I had to live off of my refund check and hope it lasted until I got paid from football. Yes, it was tough, but thanks to Jamellah and my parents I was able to manage.

The first day of classes finally came and I felt like I was prepared to get back on track. Of course, I still had to face my worst enemy thus far, calculus. I decided to take it a little later in the day and with a different professor. I already took it twice with a great professor, but I wanted to try something different. Hopefully, this change would help me pass this semester. I also took biology this semester along with a few other classes I needed. The fall semester of 2016 was my poorest semester of school ever. This semester of school made me question my abilities and drive to finish school. The highest grade I made this semester was a C. School had become an annoyance to me. I couldn't find a reason why I continued to wake up every day and drive to Francis Marion if I wasn't going to give 100% effort. Schoolwork always came easy to me, but I was not taking it seriously enough to pass any class. The only class I tried to take seriously was calculus because I knew I needed to pass this class in order to graduate in a timely manner. I went to help sessions and I even made a D on my first exam which gave me hope. It wasn't an F and I felt like I could grow from that point. That's not what happened though. The more exams I took the worse I did on them. I talked with the professor and he told me even if I made a perfect score on the final two exams, I still wouldn't pass the class. I asked him would he sign my withdraw papers to prevent me from getting another F and having three Fs from the same class on my transcript. Withdrawing from this class put me in an I don't care mood. The more I realized I wasn't doing well in calculus the more I didn't do well in other classes. I went to my biology class and took a nap every single day. There was never a day I went into his class and didn't fall asleep. One can assume I failed biology and they would be correct. I was also taking an economics class with an amazing professor. He taught me things I never knew about the community I was in and how much economics plays a role in the development of the world. The only problem was, I didn't put any time or effort into the class to pass. There I was, taking five classes for the semester. I withdrew from one that I took three times, and I got two Fs. In the other two classes I did just enough to get a C in both of them. I honestly couldn't tell you what was going through my head. Any time my family would ask me about school, I would tell them it's going great. I was working hard to make sure I got to graduation. Nobody outside of my household and Jamellah knew the struggles I was dealing with. The reality of my situation was, I couldn't blame anyone but myself.

When it was time for me to create my schedule for the next semester, I scheduled a meeting with my advisor to see what I needed. When I arrived, she looked at the grades I made in calculus and saw the withdrawal I had for the current semester. She asked me what I thought the problem was and I honestly didn't know. I told her I hadn't taken a math class in three years. She said they could put me in a pre-calculus class and that may help me get where I needed to be. The only catch was, if I took pre-calculus, I would have to stay in school for at least another three years. That was how long it would take to complete all the required math classes. She told me I needed to really sit down and think if this was the major for me. I wanted to be a math teacher for the past five years of my life. What else was there I could take and be happy with? I told her instead of making a decision that day I would go home and think about it. When I got home, I sat down with my catalog and looked through all the majors the university offered. I didn't know if I wanted to change my major or not, but I did know staying in school for another three or four years was not an option at all. Nothing jumped out to me as I looked until I got closer to the back of the book. I began to look at the psychology degree. I was always interested in psychology but majoring in it never crossed my mind because I thought I was supposed to stick with math. There weren't many extra classes I needed because I already had the majority of them even with the classes I failed. I felt like this was the best option for me and it would help me become a better coach as well. When I got to the university the next day, I went to my advisor and I told her I felt it would be best for me to change my major to something else. She was understanding and she said she was happy I found something that could work for me. Now that I had a new major, maybe my mindset would change, and I could improve my grades.

My only joy during this semester was leaving Francis Marion after I was done with classes. I was able to talk to Jamellah daily, enjoy my time with my niece, and get ready for practice. This was the first time in my life I was dreading school every morning I woke up. I wasn't taking advantage of the opportunities I had to better myself and I was prepared to throw it all away. Every day I would contemplate dropping out of school and giving it all up. The question Jamellah always asked me was, "If you drop out what are you going to do?" I had no clue as to what I would do, but I knew I didn't want to be in school anymore. There were classes where we talked about graduate school, but I was beyond certain I was done with school if I made it to graduation at Francis Marion. As that brutal semester came to a close along with football season, I really needed to decide what I wanted my future to look like. Christmas break for me was a little different this year because I had to refocus on what I wanted out of life. I was lucky enough to get a weekend job with a company that sold sports drinks while on Christmas break. This was a big relief because I still was having financial struggles. I worked there for about three months before I was fired again. The guy who hired me told me my sales weren't high enough and the company was wasting money paying me. The job wasn't all bad for me because this was when my life took a turn. One night when I got off work and was driving home, I was doing a lot of thinking. I was thinking about school, my finances, football, my family, and my future. I was lost, hurt, upset, and frustrated because my life wasn't going the way I envisioned it. I wasn't able to do some of the things I thought I should have been doing and it was really bothering me. When I was a junior in high school, I acknowledged God as my Lord and Savior, but I didn't do what was necessary to show those actions. My life felt like it was in shambles. On that night, going home by myself, I broke down in my car and for the first time since my senior year of high school, I cried. This was the first time in my life I realized I couldn't do everything on my own. Everyone is entitled to believe in whatever they want. I gave my life to Christ that night because I knew I needed help and his word would be the only thing I could lean on for the rest of my life. I didn't know what to expect from doing this, but I knew it was something I needed to do. God was the only reason I was able to accomplish the things I did and when he was not a strong factor in my life, I saw what was happening to me. This was an experience I will never forget because it changed my life for the better.

Now that I was part of the psychology department, I was optimistic about the change in majors I could find the love for school again. As the spring semester was approaching, I was ready to see how I could make a change and make sense of all the horror I was facing. This semester seemed like it would be a fresh start for me academically. The new classes would benefit my transcript and for the first time since my first semester, I was a little happy. I started the spring semester pretty strong. I was attentive and I didn't slack in my classes. However, there was one class I struggled in. Biology was my new enemy. I failed biology last semester and if I wasn't careful, I would be in the same boat this semester. Biology was never a class I found interesting and it showed because I was still dozing off in the new biology class. All of my psychology classes were going great. They were fun, interesting, and never had a dull moment. I was also minoring in economics and I was doing well in those classes too. This semester was looking promising and I was beyond excited to finally be in a good place in school again.

As the semester progressed, I was still struggling in biology. I wasn't failing the exams, but I was getting Ds. Since biology was a general education class, I needed to get a C in order to be done with it. I also began to struggle in one of my economics classes. Just when I thought there was a shining light at the end of the tunnel, it turned out to be the headlight of a train coming straight at me. I remember the day I received my fourth biology exam. All I could do was look at the grade. I knew I was going to have to retake the class again. I wasn't willing to take another class three times. I sat in the computer lab and started looking at a catalog hoping the class was offered over the summer. Unfortunately, it wasn't being offered again until the fall semester. I called Jamellah and began to explain what was going on and I told her if I didn't pass biology I was dropping out. Of course, she tried to convince me that I wasn't, but my mind was made up and I wasn't going through this again. The semester continued to move along, and finals week was approaching. I went to every study session possible to hopefully find a way to pass biology. After I took my final exam, I wasn't sure if I passed or not. I was praying something spectacular happened. About a week later the grades began to come out and it felt like an eternity. The day I checked my grades I was taking my sister, Jasmine, and her friend on a college visit. The coach offered to take us to Golden Corral which I wasn't going to turn down. As I was eating, I decided to check and see if the grades were posted. When I checked my grades somehow, I had a C in biology. I almost choked on my food, I was so stunned. I was happier than a pig in mud when I realized I passed. Sadly, I received a D in my economics class which required me to take it again, but I couldn't care less. I was elated I passed biology. This was by far the happiest moment I had at Francis Marion since I got there. It was the first time I accomplished something good towards my goal. Getting that C changed my entire perspective on finishing school. I was ready to get this journey over with.

School was officially out, and I was somewhat in a happy place. Jamellah and I went out of town for the weekend to celebrate. We had an amazing weekend to celebrate our successes and future. We were both going into our final year of college and our relationship was going well. Sunday as we were returning home, I received a phone call from my cousin, Curtis. He told me our grandfather fell out of his bed at home and when he got to the hospital, he didn't make it. Honestly, I wasn't sure how to take the news. Besides my father, my grandfather was the hardest working man I knew. This was the man we grew up idolizing because he taught us all to be men. He was in and out of the hospital a few times during the spring semester, but I knew he would pull through because I have never known him not to. He was the foundation our entire family was built on. He was the rock that kept us together and made sure everyone remained solid. It was tough to know he died because I didn't get to celebrate with him the day before. While I was in North Carolina, my family had a big gathering at my grandfather's and grandmother's house. I think about not being there often because I wasn't able to spend his last happy moments with him. This was the first major death my family ever had, and I hated that it had to be the man who made us who we are. The funeral was tough, but Jamellah was by my side the entire time and for the first time in my life I knew what real pain felt like. Time continued to move, and his death still sat with us, but in a more peaceful way. That definitely wasn't how I wanted to start my summer, but I believe God makes no mistakes.

I continued to make the best of the summer I had left. I knew I was going into my last year and I wasn't going to mess up this year. I cannot begin to tell you how excited I was about my last year of school approaching. All the happiness I was feeling got derailed when I received a letter from the registrar's office saying I was in jeopardy of losing my financial aid due to my satisfactory academic progress (SAP) percentage being under sixty-six percent. I was in college for four years and I never heard of this term before. The letter stated I needed to contact the registrar and set up a payment plan for my next semester. How was I going to pay for school and I still didn't have a job? I knew my parents weren't going to have the money for it. All those days of sleeping, not studying, and getting Fs finally caught up to me. I was less than a year away from being a college graduate and I was faced with the possibility of not being able to attend. All those times talking about dropping out were about to become a reality.

When I called the registrar, they told me I could write a letter to financial aid and explain why my grades were so low, and they may overturn the decision. However, if they gave me another chance I would be on academic probation and I couldn't fail any more classes. I was ok with those odds because I believed in my abilities. I wrote the letter and I was very honest with them. I explained where I was mentally, and I let them know I wasn't myself. I told them I was dealing with a lot in my personal life and my focus was not on being the best version of myself for school. I was blessed because they gave me another chance. I was so close to finishing, I couldn't just let it slip away from me now. I wanted to set an example for my little sister, Jasmine who was graduating this year. I wanted to let Jamellah know she wasn't going to be in a relationship with a quitter. I also wanted to make my mom and dad proud by getting a college degree.

Now that I knew I was going to officially be a senior, words couldn't express the feelings and emotions I had. I just saw all my homeboys graduate from Limestone, and I knew I couldn't let them down. I wanted to be part of that club as well. Jamellah and I were both going into our last year which made it even more exciting. She always jokes around telling me I was sweet for waiting on her. All the success that was going on around me rubbed off on me. I was forced to respond with some positivity of my own.

CHAPTER 9

TOUCHDOWN!!!

Five years later and I was finally a senior again. I didn't think I was going to make it to that point the way my last year went. Between failing classes, my grandfather dying, and receiving that letter, I was lucky to still be in school. I only had to survive two semesters and I was done with school. Nothing in the world mattered to me more than getting through my final year. I went into that year with a sense of purpose and a new mindset. I needed to make sure my grades stayed up because I was on the verge of being kicked out. I was only taking psychology and economics classes to help fulfill my major and minor. This was the first semester I had to take an online class. I never experienced it before, but if I didn't have to go into a class, I was 100% with it. I began to learn about things I never imagined. Psychology taught me about the mind and the body. It made me a better student, boyfriend, coach, and person.

There were two classes I was struggling with during this semester. The online economics class and one of my psychology classes. I wasn't in danger of failing them, but I needed to get a C to stay in good academic standing. I worked tirelessly to keep my grades where they needed to be, but the economics class was whopping me. I couldn't find a way to pass the quizzes and tests. I used every resource you could think of, but nothing helped me. The psychology class was becoming a little easier once I began to link all the classes together and study facts.

The fall semester was always a rough semester for me because being a football coach is very demanding if you want to be good at it. I practiced late and was always focusing on things to help me become a better coach and make my players better. Between school and football, I was trying to keep a balance and stay afloat in all aspects. However, just as in previous semesters, there was a wrench thrown in my path. One night in October, I was laying in my bed watching television. I received a phone call saying my cousin was shot. It was a deja vu moment for me, but definitely not expected. My mother told me he was shot, and my girlfriend called me to let me know as well. About an hour later, I received the devastating news about him dying. This was probably more hurtful than my grandfather passing because I knew it was only a matter of time for him. I knew he was having problems and as much as I would have loved for him to still be living today, I knew it was approaching for him. However, my cousin was a shock because I wasn't expecting this news at all. I was beyond angry about how he died and how things proceeded after he died. I wanted to confront his killer and everyone who played a role in it. My family told me to just relax and let everything play out. I just prayed about the situation and asked God to remove the hatred and bitterness from my heart that I had for these people. I am still a work in progress, but I am growing daily. His death hurt our entire community and it is still something I find hard to believe.

Even though his death hurt me, I knew I couldn't let it derail me from finishing strong in school. I also had to coach some players who were close to him. It was a tough situation to deal with, but we had to get through it because our lives didn't stop. I was still struggling with that economics class, but I was doing well in all my other classes. Knowing I was passing all of my classes except one was a big relief because of my past. Finals were coming up soon and I needed to do well on the remaining exams to ensure I was in a position to pass all my classes. I did as much work as I could outside of class to help me in class. As finals week got closer I knew I would have to get an A or B on my economics final exam to pass the class with a C. I started to get a little nervous because I didn't understand all the concepts we were learning and I knew my chances of making an A or B were very slim. How was I going to explain to my parents I was kicked out of school because of one class after all the craziness I had been through? I was finally taking school seriously and doing all the right things to be successful. I wasn't sure it was going to be enough to help me, but God will come through for you when you do right. In the words of Coach Danner, "If you do what you're supposed to do, the big man upstairs will throw you a bone."

Finals week was finally here, and I was prepared to take all my exams except the economics exam. I felt confident with all my psychology exams and my other economics exam. When I got in the classroom to sit down, I was beyond nervous which wasn't normal for me because I do not have testing anxiety. When I take a test, I look through the entire test front to back and read the instructions before I even write my name. This exam was no different. When he gave us the exam, I saw every student immediately begin their exam. I did my regular routine and looked through the exam to see if there was anything tricky. When I got to the final page of the exam, I couldn't believe my eyes. The professor forgot to take the answer sheet off the exam. No one in the class knew the answer sheet was on the back except me. I had two options in this scenario. I had a D average and I knew I needed to make a high grade to pass. I could have just copied the answers and turned my exam in without any worry. Or, I could get the professor's attention and let him know what he did, and I would be back at square one, not knowing enough to get an A or B. My character wouldn't allow me to keep the answer sheet. I raised my hand and asked him to come to my desk for a second and I showed him what he did. He told everyone to stop their exam and tear off the last page. Everyone was looking in shock as they realized the answer sheet was on the back. They all looked at me like I was crazy for saying anything, but I knew it was the right thing to do. When I turned my exam in, he told me he appreciated what I did because most students wouldn't have said anything, and he wouldn't forget it during final grades. When I got my final grade, he gave me a C for the class. It felt like I broke free from shackles when I saw my grades. I finally had a semester where I passed every class and didn't have to retake anything the following semester. For the first time in three years, my semester GPA was something I could show my parents and be a little proud of. I made it through the first semester of my senior year with a slight scare, but it worked out in my favor. I could enjoy my Christmas break without worrying about school for the first time in years. Knowing I had one semester left in college to be completely done was a blessing. Five years previously, I never really imagined the day I would graduate, but what other options did I have? Jamellah and I both were excited about our last semester. To make my exit a little more exciting, my sister, Jasmine decided to transfer from Morris to Francis Marion with me. She was one of the people I thought about the most when I considered dropping out because I wanted to show her it was possible. Now she would be able to see me every day, doing something she could do as well. I wanted to go out with a bang during my final semester. Making all As or at least As and Bs would make me extremely happy to finish my college career. Christmas break was coming to an end and my final semester was almost here. I was more than eager because I knew once I got this degree, I was done with school for good and I could put all this behind me.

My final semester was the best semester I had at Francis Marion. There were no distractions, and nothing deterred me from completing the task at hand. I knew I wanted to go out with a bang, and I approached every class with the mindset of passing and doing work at a high level. Nothing was going to keep me from doing my very best in every class. Before I finished the fall semester, I knew the number of classes I needed to finish, and when they were offered. I talked to my academic advisor and explained to her the classes I wanted and the times I wanted them. The only problem was I needed an extra class in economics that would interfere with another economics class I needed. Normally they do not allow you to take certain classes if you have not taken the prerequisite course or a course that could help you better understand the class. I had to meet with the director of the economics department to see if he would allow me to take the classes at the same time. Once he looked at my transcript, he told me, he didn't recommend I try and take that many classes at once because of the workload and my previous record. I told him I just needed an opportunity to finish school this semester and I would be able to handle the workload. If he didn't allow me to take the classes during the same semester, I would have to stay in school for an extra semester to finish one class. He told me again he didn't recommend me taking the class, but it was totally up to me. I thanked him and was ready to set my schedule. An issue came in because one of the economics classes was only offered during the time of a psychology class I needed as well. Luckily, my advisor found out the psychology class was being offered online. Taking that class online would free up the time slot for the economics class. I was all set to take my classes and get ready for graduation.

All the classes I had were learning experiences and taught me about the real world. I was confident every day I went into my classes. This was the semester I started going to job fairs and getting my resume prepared for the workforce. My grades were great and the classes I was taking were great. There was one obstacle I was facing during this semester. The director of the economics department was my professor. His class was the class I was having trouble in. What a coincidence this was. I was passing every class with As and Bs except his. He was a great professor, but there was some stuff I didn't do up to par on the exams we took. I begged him to let me take both of the economic classes because I could handle it and now, I was struggling in his class.

We only had four exams in his class and then we had to take the final exam. I did okay on the four exams, but I wasn't doing well enough to not be worried. I was passing my other classes with flying colors. I received an email saying I needed to apply for graduation and pay the graduation fees to ensure I would be prepared when the time came. The only problem was I wasn't sure if I would be graduating or not depending on my final grade in this economics class. Worried was an understatement for how I felt. I needed to pass this class and my professor wasn't giving any information on my grade. I wasn't sure if I was passing or not, but I got prepared for graduation as if I already passed. I knew I was going to pass all my other classes and the final exams for those classes. When it was time to take the final, I wasn't nervous, but I knew what was at risk for me. I took the exam with confidence and waited with anticipation to see the outcome. The grades didn't come out until one or two days before graduation. There was no way I was going to wait that long to know if I passed. I sent my professor an email to ask him about my grade and he told me I had to wait until grades were released. I waited, what seemed to be an eternity, but by the grace of God, I passed with a C. When I officially knew I was graduating, I was overwhelmed with emotion. I didn't cry, but there was a joy that came over me I couldn't explain. Everyone in my house was excited for me because they knew the journey I took to get to this point.

On the day of graduation, I was the first student there. I waited for an hour or two just to have a chance to bask in the achievement of making it to this point. Despite the trials and mishaps I had during my tenure at Francis Marion, I made it to the finish line. My economics professor saw me in the hallway and joked around with me, saying he wanted me to be worried. None of the grades I got mattered at that point because I made it through college. When I was finally able to hear my name called and I walked across that stage, it felt like I won a championship game on the final play. Being able to see my mom and dad smile and congratulate me was the best feeling in the world. My sisters, niece, and my girlfriend were all there to help me celebrate as well. I was happy to accomplish this goal because I was the first one in my house to do it. I was even happier because I got a chance to see my girlfriend do the same thing the following weekend. We were both college graduates and ready for the next steps in our lives.

I wasn't sure what would be next for me, but I knew I was finally free of school, and going back was not an option. I needed to find a job and start making some money for myself. My summer was dedicated to finding a job and coaching football. Now that I had a degree to go along with a good resume, I was prepared to enter the workforce full throttle. I was officially ready to start adulthood and create new adventures and experiences for myself. As I learned throughout my journey, your plans are never really your plans. God always has the final word on your journey. I was fortunate to receive a job as a special education teacher which I have been doing for three years now. I am currently going into my fifth year as a high school football coach and my fourth year as a high school baseball coach. I am engaged to my girlfriend, Jamellah of nine years. Although I hated school more than anyone I ever met, I now have a Master of Science in Education as well. I am currently looking at other graduate programs to possibly receive another master's degree or a doctoral degree for the future. I have overcome my financial struggles and found inner peace.

Despite the obstacles I faced and the strain I put on myself, I never let my failures win. Every day I wake up, I think about how far I have come, and I can honestly say my failures are my motivation for success. I am still working to make an impact in the world and leave a legacy behind. God guides me every day and I am blessed to be in a position to take care of my family and help others as well. Always remember, failure is part of the success, and it's not about how many times you fail, but how many times you get up from failures. Keep hustling, persevere, stay committed, and BOSS UP!!!

Pure Thoughts Publishing, LLC